T0115060

DANCE
OF THE
DARK SKINNED GIRL

DANCE OF THE
DARK SKINNED GIRL

C SMITH

authorHOUSE®

AuthorHouse™
1663 Liberty Drive
Bloomington, IN 47403
www.authorhouse.com
Phone: 1-800-839-8640

Published by AuthorHouse   12/19/2012

ISBN: 978-1-4772-9324-9 (sc)
ISBN: 978-1-4772-9323-2 (e)

Library of Congress Control Number: 2012922021

This book is dedicated to my family, my brothers and sisters. My mother is has gone on, who always encouraged me in every phase of my life. To my three children: Nichelle, Natasha, and Samuel, whom I love with all my heart. For their ability to make me laugh in the most desperate situations, I thank you. To my special friend who always told me (if not in this life than the next). In addition, most importantly, to my King for changing my life and giving your love, I give thanks. In the process of finishing this book I lost my sister and friend, Phyllis I miss you greatly. Special thanks to Drew for posing as me on the cover of the book.

Special thanks to Aleex Conner who did the cover of the book, and Arthur Smith who did the last picture in the book a dark skinned dancer. It is my hope that this short story of my life will encourage another girl or boy to have faith in God, and dance on. You are not alone.

DANCE OF THE DARK SKINNED GIRL

For as long as I could remember, someone always referred to me according to my complexion, whether black or white. It was never by name but I was described in terms of color. I never understood when I was younger what this meant, but when I became older, it struck me why do people do that, even today I hate saying the white girl did this or the black girl did that. I rather say the blond hair woman with the beautiful smile, or the nice man who was so pleasant. My first encounter to the reference of my complexion and the connection to some imperfection occurred many years ago, but I will talk about that later. To set the tone for this book and the time I will describe people in terms of color. This is only to set the stage for the era of time I am referring too.

I lived in a southern mid Atlantic town, with many other black families in a middle class neighborhood; I believe we were the poorest family on that block. Growing up the only white face I saw was the insurance man who visited each household on Saturday mornings. The other white man that came to our house was a man who carried a sack containing small whatnots, which my mother collected and placed in various places around the house. I wish I had saved some of those trinkets, I am sure they are probably worth more today, than back then. My mother was a quiet mannered woman, somewhat timid, and she never discussed race with her family. Neither was race mentioned in my family, at least I never heard that conversation. I was the youngest of five children; I had been called a second-generation child, since my brothers and sisters were in high school when I was born.

My earliest memory occurred when I was three years old, my father was leaving my mother, I remember him packing a U-Haul truck and attaching it to the back of his care. The last thing he did was hand me a ball, and I watched him drive off. From that point on, I do not remember him being around our home often, my memory is patchy about him until I started attending middle school. He would occasionally drop in on us when I needed something important for school, or if I had a discipline problem, which my mother felt he needed to handle.

The night my father left our house, the atmosphere of my environment changed there was a lot of laughter and my siblings had a party, our home became very loud, with many unfamiliar voices. My oldest brother placed me in my crib and gave me a bottle of water to drink; he was always attentive to me. I laid in the dark of my room listening to the laughter roaring up from the basement, two flights down. I didn't know for years the cause for my siblings happiness, and how it related to my father's departure. Many years after I had grown up I learned to understand why my siblings where so joyous about his leaving.

My neighborhood was filled with generational black families who had saved their monies to buy these large row homes. The men on my block where hard working, some of them post Korean War veterans. As was my father and as a benefit for serving in that war, he was one of the first black men in our area to be hired by the U.S. postal service. My house was a large brick semi-detached home, separated on the right side by a small alley, which led to my back yard. Our home was in need of a great deal of repair, and after my father left, my mother did not have the means to pay for maintenances. As for calling my father to help in the repair, and I cannot say that he ever put me in mind of a handy man. He was always very neat, even down to his shoes. I can say until the day he died, I never saw his tennis shoes with dirt on them. To enter my home one had to be careful, the front porch was very unstable. With one false move you could fall through. Only one body could walk down at a time and be comfortable in a narrow hallway. To the right of the hallway was a small room, if it was not for the furniture there, you would wonder what benefit this room served. It was a living room, so small that conventional furniture did not fit inside. However, my mother managed to get two sofas in that small space. Outside of the living room was a large foyer, with a mirror mounted on the wall, and a telephone bench at the foot of the stairs. On the other side of the foyer was the large dining room, which led to a kitchen, and a pantry with a stove squeezed into it. Off the kitchen was a wooden back porch with no stairs you either climbed or jumped down. As a child, I was not allowed to go on the back porch because of the danger. As I grew older, I remember hearing stories of how different family friends would jump off the porch to escape my father's arrival at home. The backyard was overgrown with grass, but occasionally one of my brothers would borrow a push mower and cut the grass. The house would have been a designer's dream, but for us money was a dream. I never knew how much help my father gave to my mother. I do know my mother worked three jobs to make ends meet. Every day during the week, she would leave the house about 5:30 am and would not return home until 9:30 pm. She would awaken me every morning about 5:00am to fix my hair; I would then go back to sleep until the alarm woke me up. She always looked very exhausted to me, when she arrived home, but when the weekend came she would rest. Times with my mother where very special, even as a child I was aware she had little time to share. Once a month my mother would take me on a trolley car to a famous down town drug store. She would order me a cheeseburger, fries and a chocolate shake. It never occurred to me until years later we always sat in the same place in the back of the diner. The same very small white woman would wait on our table she was always pleasant to my mother and me. I was just happy to be with my mother, that simple monthly outing meant the world to me. My mother had a very distinct laugh, which would make you stop whatever you were doing and laugh with her. She would bellow loud hit a high peak and come back down, with an oooh child as if she had run a race and was at the finish line. On Saturday evenings, my mother and our next-door neighbor a younger women than my mother would sit out on the concrete steps and sip a beer. My mother was not a drinker; she nursed that one beer all night. I believe she held it in her hand just to be sociable.

I believe on these evening the weight of the world was temporarily off her shoulders at least for the weekend.

In the summer of 1960 the temperatures where hotter than usual, I was seven years old at that time. I would sit on those concrete steps and watch the coming and goings of my neighbors. Under my mother's orders, I was not allowed to leave those hard steps and if I did, it was only to walk to the edge of the walkway and come back to the steps. Most of my neighbors where sitting on their porches as well or in their living rooms near the front of the house, because air conditioning did not exist in the houses on my street. As you walk down the street, you could see the multitude of fans sitting in the windows, and all the windows that face the street wide open. One day in that hot summer, I noticed my neighbor across the street and his male friend arguing. I had seen them together on numerous occasions, but never like this. The words between them began to grow louder and louder so that sitting across the street I could understand every word spoken. Suddenly one of the men pulled out a knife and they began to struggle, from their door front across the street. Somehow the fight ended up right in front of my door, as I stood on the steps frightened. Then one of them stabbed the other, one of my neighbors must have called the police, who pulled up in front of my door, followed by the ambulance. The injured man was taken by ambulance and the other was led away by the police. I never knew whether the man survived the injury, I never saw him or the other man again. With all the excitement, the neighborhood was a buzz of what caused the fight, with some speculations that the wife had caused it. I was fascinated with the blood on the concrete pavement in front of my house. While everyone else was talking, I counted the drops of blood on the ground; I had never seen anything like this before. For the rest of the summer I had lost my curiosity to get off the concrete steps. I felt safe playing close to my broken porch or kick ball in the alley next to my house.

Finally, fall came and it was time for me to return to school, I was going into the second grade, and I experienced walking to school all alone, school was four long blocks away. The first few days I walked alone, then I noticed the children who lived next door to me were going the same way. These were the children of my mother's friend whom she would sit on steps with on Saturday evenings. There were four of them two boys and two girls. The oldest of the four children was a boy in junior high, and the rest of the children were in elementary school. He would walk them to school first and go straight to the school he attended. Since they were going my way, I decided to tag along with them. The beginning of the school year went well, but in the fall, a boy named Mad Dog would harass us daily from his bicycle. He would stop us on the way to school, and often confront the oldest boy to entice him into a fight, but we would just keep walking. The other children seemed to know him and became frightened when they saw him. Immediately it was becoming serious, he began taking our books and throwing them. When we took our dolls to school for show and tell, he would take them and stomp on them. Now getting to school became a covert operation, and going to school in fear frightened me even more than the knife fight I had seen earlier that year. By the end of that school year word came that a child had been hit by a car and killed on his bicycle. Word somehow came to me that it was Mad Dog, it is sad to say we breathed a little easier the rest of the school year. I did not comprehend what death was I just knew it meant no coming back. During this time of the school year I was having issues with my teacher, and it was evident to them I had some learning difficulties. My lack of confidence and my shyness was now affecting my ability to function in school. When I was called to the blackboard, it was a crippling feeling; I would rather face torture than to stand in front of a class. My teacher had enough of my lack of participation. This caused her to call my mother, in which she was informed of my possible learning disability. My shyness also disturbed my capability to participate in sports with the other children, so I was never chosen for teams. My introvert behavior somehow made me very clumsy and unable to balance myself properly. If I had to do anything in front of an audience I would fall or fold like a deck of cards, unable to complete any task. I did pass from second into the third grade, but my teacher conveyed great concern to my mother.

Finally, the summer came again and I was free from school, teachers', students, and the need to perform tasks in front of others. I could once again entertain myself in front of my mirror without worry, I enjoyed being alone. One of my greatest joys then was pretending in the mirror in the foyer. I usually pretended I was a ballerina. My family had a large collection of old classic records, my father had left when he moved. I would play them while I pretended to dance before my fake audiences, and bow in the mirror at the end of my solo performances. During this summer, I also started to sing to jazz recordings, like Billie Holiday, and Ella Fitzgerald's "A Tisket A Tasket." The summer went by quickly, and for all children it seemed as if the fall came too quickly. Before the next school year began, my mother received a letter from the school board stating a new elementary school was opening up two blocks from our home. Beginning in the fall semester half of the children would be transferred to this new school. The new elementary school would be called Beltsville Elementary, and it would be a closer walk to school for the children who lived in my neighborhood. This meant I would get home from school sooner and I would need a baby sitter. The thought of going to someone's home or having them come into mine just to watch me was uncomfortable. My mother's normal routine was to leave the house at 5:15 am and return to the house about 9:15 pm. She worked a full time job and two part time jobs. When school first began she asked her girlfriend next door, the mother of the four children I walked to school with to watch me. I will always remember Mrs. Martha, who was so different from my own mother. She was a very jazzy woman, who always dressed well, and was always singing. I can still hear her singing one of my favorite songs by Dinah Washington "What a Difference a Day Makes." She began to notice the shyness in me and would place a mirror in front of me and tell me, there was nothing wrong with the way I looked. "Why do you believe you are ugly," she would question me. To me there had to be something different about me, I was not comfortable around people like other kids. Mrs. Martha attempted to build some confidence in me, and I am ever grateful for the time she spent with me. I enjoyed being around her and would attempt to imitate her and the artist songs she sang. For the first time in my life from Mrs. Martha I realized what a complete family was like, eating around a table together with open conversation there, a father present in the home, and the sound of his voice calling the other kids fascinated me. I found myself going over there to be with them even when Mrs. Martha was not babysitting me. I guess it was too much for her husband though, because one day he suggested I stay at my own house sometimes. So I stopped going over there, I never told my mother or Mrs. Martha why I stopped coming over.

In the fall, the school year began and my new school was huge compared to my previous elementary school. We began our school day with an introduction to our new principal. She was the tallest women I had ever seen, and the sound of her voice matched her stature. Her name was Mrs. Baylor and her presence struck fear in our hearts. I was starting the third grade along with other children who had transferred from various schools. Most of the children were new to each other, although some lived in the same neighborhoods. Under Mrs. Baylor, the school was run like a military camp. She laid down the rules in the very first assembly. There would be no talking at all in the auditorium for any reason; no running in the halls and an orderly line must be kept while you are waiting to be served in the cafeteria. The cafeteria line was a long winding line, and very orderly as Mrs. Baylor commanded. I did appreciate the wait, because Mrs. Baylor always played jazz and relaxing music while we waited. The whole atmosphere in the line was calming and peaceful. I came to appreciate many jazz artists, thanks to Mrs. Baylor's taste in music, especially Jackie Gleason, whom I still listen too.

After the first week in school, we had an assembly in which the local college was to perform. They announced the name of the college, and I turned to the girl next to me, and said my brother goes there. Immediately hands touched my shoulder, and the shoulder of the girl next to me. I only wanted to express my pride in an older brother. Mrs. Baylor than signaled me to follow her to the office. I had learned the rules at the first assembly so when Mrs. Baylor questioned me about talking I denied it. Unfortunately the girl next to me denied talking as well. Mrs. Baylor said nothing else to either of us; she just went into her office, as we sat in the office chairs. Soon after my mother arrived at the principal's office, Mrs. Baylor informed my mother that I was to be suspended for three days for lying to her. My mother looked at me so disappointed, because she was unable to take the time off from work. So my mother called my father and I was in my room when he arrived to give me my first spanking. He informed me that this would hurt him more than me.

I never understood that statement; it was a short spanking, but memorable. My father never spanked me again, but I was to spend those three days with him. After those three days were complete, I returned to my mirror in the foyer of my house. The incident at school caused me to go deeper into my shell of imagination and I could not wait until the school semester ended.

Every morning before going to school, I would pick out my own clothes to wear, I had no sense of style and color. I just put on what was easiest and went on my way. During this school year, girls my age were beginning to notice what they wore and what you wore. This was going to be a problem for me. The summer came and went too quickly, and I was now in the fourth grade. This was the beginning of many new lessons for me, and I was about to change. In the fourth grade my morning ritual remained the same, my mother still awakened me at 5:15am to comb my hair and I went back to sleep until the alarm sounded. She still combed my hair into two plaits in the back of my head and one in the front of my hair. By the time I awakened in the morning for school, the front plait was sticking straight up, and the back two were pointing in different angles.

My new fourth grade teacher was a very large woman both in height and in width. The boys in my class learned discipline from this teacher. Her name was Mrs. Flechman, and she would sit on the boys who got out of hand. The whole class was very attentive and well behaved because of the punishment we witnessed. We had a lot of incentives for excellent behavior. This school year Mrs. Baylor decided to start an extra circular enhancement-reading program. She chose a student from every fourth grade class; from Mrs. Flechman's group I was selected. Once a week we were to meet Mrs. Baylor in her private office to enjoy a special time of reading, and discuss our thoughts on the stories presented. The first week when I was to report to Mrs. Baylor's office, before I could attend, Mrs. Flechman called me to the front of the classroom. I had been in school all morning and had not noticed how I looked, I never did. Once I reported to Mrs. Flechman, she pointed out that my hair was flying in several directions. She began to lecture me on the importance of looking well before going to the principal's office.

Then she proceeded to comb my hair in front of the class. This ritual continued, every Wednesday, for weeks. I attempted to fix my own hair just so I could be spared the humiliation of being in front of the class. I felt worse than I ever had about myself, because children can be so hard on each other from what they learn or see. My classmates also began to chime in on my appearance. Not only was my hair the topic of conversation, so were my clothes, and the way I dressed. There is nothing worse than when a teacher harasses you, and the children continue the program.

Things were getting worse because my mother decided I needed another baby sitter. The woman next door volunteered for the job. I had seen the woman all my life, but she had never kept me on a regular basis. What I hated about this woman's house was her black poppy-eyed dog, which would bite you either on the way in or on the way out of her house. She was a very kind woman who had several foster children. Her husband was a very nice, easygoing gentle man who liked to hunt. Whatever he killed, he would bring it home and carve it on his cutting board. I never saw them eat what he had killed, at least I believe we had never eaten anything he killed while I was under her care. She or her husband was always cooking, and when I arrived from school, one of them was always in the kitchen. They were from the deep south and always had relatives visiting, their home. One afternoon while in her home her nephew approached me. I had seen him there on several occasions, a man in his twenties or thirties, and he really did not talk much, so I did not pay attention to him. While I was watching the television he suddenly came up behind me, threw a bucket over my head, and began to touch my breast. I began to defend myself and he hurried out of the room. I became so frightened that I lied to the babysitter and told her my mother had come home early. I ran out of her house and stayed in the alley next to my house where no one could see me. One of my brothers came home, and I went to the house with him. I was so upset about what happened that I did not tell him or my mother when she arrived home. I just began to beg my mother to allow me to stay home in the evenings by myself, because I was old enough to be trusted alone. I told my mother if anything happened I would run next door and get my neighbor if I needed anything. My mother was still uncomfortable with the idea of me home alone, so she made one more attempt to place me in someone's care. She talked to the woman who did her hair; who had a teenage daughter who wanted to earn some extra money. The family lived two doors down from us. This arrangement turned out to be a disaster. For some reason I rubbed this girl the wrong way immediately. She had some mental health issues, which came out only a few days after I started staying with her. One day she made a comment about my mother, I do not remember what she said, so I in turn said "I hope your mother becomes ill," and asked her not to talk about my mother. Suddenly the girl grabbed me around the throat and began to choke me; her brother ran in and pulled this almost grown teenager off me. This was it for me no more babysitters, I decided my mother had to listen to me about this situation. When my mother arrived home that night, I pleaded with her to allow me to have a key to the front door, and before going to bed, she agreed. The plan my mother had come up with, was that I was to report to the woman next door when I arrived home from school. Once I had gotten in to the house I could make myself a sandwich, and before the streetlights came on I could walk down to the end of the block to Kleinfield's store for my favorite oatmeal cookies. My mother would now leave me five cents to buy five cookies from Kleinfield's store every night before she got home. I could stroll down to the end of the block and feel safe, because I knew most of my neighbors watched every child on my street. They were always ready to give the parent an account of every action the child had done, or a spanking if the child got out of line. My first week home alone was going smooth, until I saw the nephew, of the woman next door, sitting on the porch. He sat there so calmly as if he had done nothing. I began to draw horrible pictures of him and pasted them to the front window, knowing he saw them. Hoping he would get the idea to leave the porch, it was the only way I knew to fight him back. After that, I did not see him as much. Every day after school I continued to dance in my mirror, with no one to bother me, it was the best part of the day. After my dance I would make myself a mayonnaise sandwich, occasionally I would have bologna if we had any. The highlight of my evening was the walk to Kleinfield's store for my oatmeal cookies.

Things at school had not changed I continued to go through the same process every Wednesday, from Mrs. Flechman, no matter how much I attempted to fix my hair, it was never good enough for her. One week I became very ill, I am still unsure of what the problem was; only that I was out of school for several days, and I was happy. The medication had caused my lips to develop sores and they were grossly swollen. When I returned to school it was a terrible time because the children at school shunned me as if I embodied someone with a deforming disease that was contagious. Children will be children, and for that week, the other students where brutal towards me and if one touched me that would mean certain death. The lunch line was worse, there was a large space in front of and behind me, and there I was in the middle. I soon became the brunt of the jokes around school; even the outcast students mustered up some bravery by making insults toward me. In all schools various nicknames stick, we had students especially boys who were known as the pissy ones, or smelly children, I was now known as the girl with the diseased lips. This whole incident caused me to withdraw in a very deep shell; it became very hard now for me to participate in any school activities. My mother started receiving phone calls from my teachers, especially my gym teacher concerning my performance. One day after the lip disaster, my physical education teacher requested the class to walk across the balance beam. Every student in the class had to take turns on the beam; there I stood in line, hoping to vanish, but the line in front of me kept getting shorter. Finally, it was my turn and the whole class fixed their eyes on me. As I mounted the balance beam, I felt there, eyes upon me with every step I made on the beam. I just could not do it, on the third step I fell off the beam with grace of an elephant. The children in the class erupted into laughter. In addition, of course the class added some personal details about my lips and hair, as if these shortcomings had caused me to fall. This was my life in elementary school in 1964. Some of the girls in my fourth grade class felt it there duty to harass me, by confronting me, pushing me around, and of course loud talking me. This loud talking was done to attract others to come over, I was like a wounded animal now, and I had to defend myself in some way. This oppressive behavior toward me went on for several days. The ringleader of this group was named Irene, and she had a reputation for being wild and tough in our school.

One Friday evening as usual, I went down to Kleinfields store to purchase my five oatmeal cookies, as I came out of the store Irene and her gang where coming into the store. They immediately began to push at me, I allowed them to push me, and I just backed up protecting my bag of oatmeal cookies. Suddenly Irene snatched the bag from me, threw my cookies to the ground, and stomped on the bag. I lost whatever innocence I had, I jumped on her like a cowboy holds down a calf to brand it. Hair began flying and I do not remember much after that, only that she left the store crying along with her girlfriends I ran home because it was so dark, hoping my mother had not found out about the fight. I suddenly notice it was pass 9:30 and my mother was not home. First the fight with Irene, my mother wasn't home and I was still alone. My mind began to race, "what if this was the way it was going to be, no mother, me by myself?" I fell on my knees and prayed like the picture we had in the house of a figure praying toward the heavens. I asked God, "could you send my mother home safely." At about 9:45 my mother came through the door, I ran and hugged her, and she looked at me with a surprised look on her face. I knew at that time I could pray and my prayers could be answered. At that time, we did not attend a church. As she sat down on the sofa I did tell her about the fight, but she was so tired I do not think she heard me, so I just laid my head on her breast and rested with her on the sofa.

The next week of school the news had spread about the fight between Irene and I, I noticed some of the kids at school looked at me a bit differently. They still did not accept me, but they considered I could fight one of them and win, so they left me alone, and I was okay with that. School became very peaceful in the following weeks, no one bothered me and I stayed to myself. Not long after my weeks of peace my mother came home early and asked me to change my clothes and come with her. We had to walk six blocks because we had no transportation. We arrived at a school that I was not familiar with.

We entered the school from the back, and went straight into the gymnasium; there my mother's friend met us. They both escorted me into the gym area, where there were about 25 girls of all ages and sizes. Some of the girls where tap-dancing, others were doing modern dance or jazz. My mother turned to me and asked if I would like to join and come on Tuesdays and Thursdays, to this school. I wanted to take off running, dancing in front of strangers was something completely different for me. The following Thursday was a long day for me, I thought about the dance program all day. I knew after school I would walk the six blocks to that new dance program. I walked as fast as I could to be there on time, just as I was about to approach the school I saw a familiar face. It was my Papa John sitting outside of the local barbershop. As I approached him I heard him say 'here is a quarter little girl, I see you made it." My Papa John always had a large cigar hanging out the side of his mouth and I loved the smell of the brand he smoked. He was a very tall gentle man, who was one of the best cooks I knew. He would cure bacon in his basement, and could make the best rolls I have ever tasted. His rolls where so good, on Sundays people would come to my grandparents' home from various places in the city to buy them. I am sorry to this day I never asked my Papa John how he made those rolls.

That first day in the gym, I watched all of the other girls dancing to different music with different interpretations of the music they heard. One girl appeared to be one of the main dancers she was the daughter of my mother's friend. As she came on to the stage, all the other girls stopped what they were doing to watch her. She danced so well that during her performance, the teachers stopped to watch her dance, and when she had completed her presentation the whole room applauded. I stood there mesmerized, while one of the teachers approached me, and asked what type of music I would like to dance to. I looked at her and thought after seeing that demonstration of dance I would try all types of music. During rehearsals, I would try to be on the end in the back of the line, so if I messed up it would go unnoticed. After dance practice when I arrived home, I would dance in my mirror. I could recall all the steps and the music we would perform to. I would even make up my own dance routines to the music. I now attended the afternoon dance classes regularly on Tuesdays and Thursdays. On each of these days I would always run into my Papa John who would be standing outside of the barbershop with a quarter in his hand, During dance class I continued to stand in the back row, far on the end of the line to keep from being noticed. We had completed 4 weeks of rehearsals, and it was not time or money wasted. The recital was to show parents this was not a wasted investment. The parents were informed what costumes to purchase for the recital. I remember this posed a difficult challenge for my mother who did not have the money for this. I remember her calling my father and pleading for assistance. I understood in later years my mother felt this might be a way to bring me out of the shell I was in, so she was determined to help me any way she could. I hated to see her so upset about this, I was okay with just watching the other girls from the audience, but it meant a lot to my mother. So I determined in my mind I would do my best even from the back row in the corner. My mother finaly convinced my father to purchase my costume. She thought this was just the activity I needed, to give me some confidence. I hated to see her so upset about the recital, it was okay with me if we just went together and watched the other dancers perform but I also wanted my mother to be proud of me.

That night the gym was pack to capacity filled with parents, grandparents, and just people from the neighborhood. I had never seen so many people in one place. These were the days when black people came together to support each other, no matter the cause. The girl who was the star did a solo performance to Gold Finger; the teachers had sprayed her with gold paint over her black leotard, after her performance the audience jumped to their feet. I loved her style of dance but the music did not make me want to dance as other music I had heard. As the administrator for the dance school came to the podium she thanked all the participants, she was accompanied by a very tall light-skinned beautiful girl. She had been a previous student of the afterschool dance class, and now had moved on to professional dancing. She demonstrated her ability to stand on her toes which I had never seen before. She then spread her arms out like a bird beginning to take flight, such grace was new to me. I was very impressed, and I thought to myself if I am going to dance, this is what I want to be like. The last dance on stage was with every class on stage at the same time. I found my place at the end of the line in the corner, but I saw my mother's eyes directly on me watching every step I made. When it was over I walked home with my mother, she placed her arm around me, and I knew that she was very proud.

The end of the school year had finally come and I barely made it out of the fourth grade. This was the summer I would meet death personally for the first time. My introduction would come through my grandmother. My grandmother was a woman who made it clear her heritage did not include dark skinned people, she hated my father because of his complexion. My history with my grandmother was not a deep relationship, as others may have with their grandmothers. My memory of her was my family going to her house, she would cook, the food was very delicious, and me sitting on the living room sofa until supper was prepared. She was not a very loving woman, I suppose, but I spent the least amount of time with her. My memory of her was her giving me one chocolate and telling me to sit on the sofa, and she commented that I was getting taller. There was no holding or rocking or any love from her toward me. I guess by the time I was born she was tired.

This particular week my brothers and sister stayed home from their jobs and activities at my mother's request. It was a Thursday evening the whole family was in mommies' room with my grandmother. My mother and siblings helped her down stairs, that is when I realized something was wrong, she acted as if she did not recognize me.

They left for another room to talk about something, and I was left alone with my grandmother. Suddenly she stood up and walked out of the front door, I stood there watching her, when my mother came back and asked where she was, I told her she left. Every one ran out of the door, and in a few minutes, they brought her back to the house.

My mother and my brother put my grandmother in the car and left. I am not sure where they went, but the house's atmosphere had changed. My mother did not return home that night and I was alone with one of my sisters. The phone rang and I will remember that scream for as long as I live, she kept yelling she's dead she's dead, drop the phone and ran out of the house. I just stood there wondering what does dead mean. I followed her and ran to the porch, only to see the neighbors bring my sister back inside and calm her down. I sat down in front of my mirror and cried, because my sister cried. The following day I overheard my brother and mother arguing, my brother believed I was too young to attend a funeral, he pleaded with my mother saying I was not ready to be exposed to death, and this may drive me deeper into my shell.

At the end of the week, my house was overcrowded with people I had never seen before. My famous disc jockey uncle came he was also a man of few words like my grandmother. He looked at me as I leaned on his car, and told me to get off it. Fortunately toward the end of his life we began to talk and became friends. That morning my mother dressed me and she had the women down the street to straighten my hair. I did not look as I usually did; I was dressed up in my new pink and white dress. My father even came over that morning. We all got into a long black car with several rows of seats. My eyes were glued to my mother I could see the sadness in her face. As we walked into the church we all sat down on the front pew, my brother held my hand tight, while my mother attempted to keep herself and my sisters calm. The final call came from the minister, and they rolled the casket over to the front row. My hand became tighter in my brothers hand; I cried because, my mother cried, I looked down at my grandmother, who looked peacefully asleep, she had on pink just like me. The following Sunday morning my mother asked us to get a pan of rolls from my Papa John's house. I still have not tasted rolls like his since his death. This summer had been especially hard on my mother because of financial stress and my grandmother's death. She looked worried most of the time. She came to me and told me she had no money to buy me anything new this coming school year.

I was not upset because clothing did not really mean that much to me. The week before school was to begin my aunt from New York called and asked my mother to come for the weekend, just to help get her mind off her troubles. Friday we caught a bus to New York and I loved it. I was very excited about eating in a bus terminal for the first time.

There was something about the bus terminal cafeteria-style food, it had a certain delightful smell, which even today, if I pick up the sweet savory scent, I think of my mother. The aunt we visited was my mother's younger sister, and she was a bit eccentric, she was a model in her younger years. She had a beautiful slender build; and she looked much younger than she was. She knew about beauty and wore the beautiful wigs all the time, in fact I never saw my aunt's real hair, but mother told me it was beautiful. When she got up in the morning with her wig on, which was before weaves, it was a real mystery to me. One day she decided to speak to me about my looks, she would say "you have a good profile," I did not understand what she meant, so I asked my mother, who told me a profile is when you turn your head to the side and people only see the side of your face. From then on when I wanted to impress people, I let them see the side of my face. Now when I look back on this behavior, I believe people thought I was strange. I had a great time in New York, although my uncle and aunt where strange people, I enjoyed the change, the subway, the delicatessens, bakeries, and freedom land right across the street with it's nightly fireworks.

When we arrived home late that Sunday evening getting out of the cab, I saw a man standing in the shadows, beside our house. He called my mother by name, as we approached him I noticed my mother began to smile, I thought to myself, is this a lost relative or someone who knew us. He just began to count out money to my mother, one hundred, and so on up to one thousand dollars. My mother turned to me and said we have some school shopping to do.

That night I could not explain it but I could feel a change in the air for me, a feeling that something was changing in me. Then school began, it was the final stage for elementary school, the sixth grade. I went in to my room assignment and met Miss Berkley a beautiful light skinned women, about 5 feet 7 inches, the way she carried herself I knew she had to be a model. I watched her every movement that day, she walked with such elegance and poise. She was very soft spoken but stern. She went around the room to meet each classmate and asked each of us to give our name. As she approached me, I wanted to place my best foot forward, so I gave her the profile and said my name. Understandably, she looked at me strangely as if something may be wrong with me, and then moved on to the next student. After a month in school, Miss Berkley sent out letters to hold a parent—teacher conference. My mother was unable to attend so my older brother came in my mother's stead. Miss Berkley was so beautiful my brother started talking to her, since his major in college was teaching; I believe he forgot about me. Miss Berkley seemed to have that effect on most men, even other male teachers in the school. This school year was very critical because of the test at the end of the year. In our school system if you did not pass the state examination, you could not enter junior high school until you did. At this point in the school year my grades where fair, but if I was put under I would crumble like tin foil. That whole school year there were tests after tests, in preparation for the big test. By the end of the school year letters went home to parents regarding test scores, my test scores were not encouraging. It seems I could not get a passing grade on these standardized tests. At the end of the school year Miss Berkley's dance group gave a recital, they were called the Magnificent Seven; they were a beautiful group of sixth grade girls. As I watched them perform I began to think to myself I could be up on stage dancing with them. There were not any steps they performed that seemed difficult to me. When I got home, I would repeat all the steps I saw in my mirror. Later on that evening I had made up my mind after the holiday, I would ask Miss Berkley if I could join the dance group. The only person I told about my plan was my girlfriend Sharon and she expressed her disapproval of the idea. She tried daily to talk me out of it, than she told me I was too dark to dance with those light-skinned girls. I yelled back at her we are all negroes.

For some time Sharon and I parted ways and I had to admit I was lonely without her, but something deep inside kept pushing me to pursue my idea. I felt if I could just accomplish one thing without failing I could do more. Over the school break, my mother had a talk with me about my grades on the test, and my need to do better, when the next test was given. If I did not pass the examination I would have to repeat the sixth grade. I remember the worry in her face; I assured her I would work hard to pass the test. When school started back once again, twice a week I attended the after school dance program. I missed seeing my Papa John on the corner, the other men who stood on the corner with my Papa John did speak to me; one of the men gave me a quarter just like he did. The next day was Wednesday and I knew Miss Berkley and her dance group would be rehearsing. I waited in the back of the auditorium, until rehearsal was over. Then I approached Miss Berkley. When I was in her classroom, I got the impression she thought I was slightly mentally retarded. I felt I did not have a chance, because this teacher did not really communicate with me. I also felt if I did not try, something on the inside would die. I quietly sat beside her and as she began to take off her tap shoes and the other girls where in the back room changing. I asked Miss Berkley if I could join the dance group, she stared at me as if I spoke in a foreign tongue. She then repeated my words, "can you join the group," she laughed then continued changing her shoes. I told her I could dance too, then she knew I was serious. She stared at me for a few minutes, so I gave her my profile as sort of a convincing statement. By this time, some of the dance group had emerged from the back room, and they watched from the stage the conversation-taking place. She then turned to me and said "I tell you what, one month from today you come to our rehearsal and dance a solo and we will decide if you can join our group." As I was leaving the auditorium I could hear some of the dance group laughing in the background, and one of the girls stated "she can not even comb her hair how can she dance."

The walk home seemed longer than usual, all the way home I kept thinking maybe Sharon was right, I do not belong in that group. If I could dance in front of them as well as I danced in my home mirror, I could get into the group. The next day word had spread around the school like wild fire. Children in every classroom from the fourth to the sixth grades were talking about the upcoming performance. Most of my classmates felt I was out of my mind to even attempt or think about entering the group. As I walked to dance class that evening, a familiar voice came up behind me. Sharon asked me what dance I would do, had I picked out any music. She felt it had to be out of this world, something that would knock them off their feet. Two weeks had passed and I had no ideas of what type of dance I would do, or the music I would use. We continued taking practice tests for the big final, and my grades on the practice examination had not improved either.

One day at my Thursday afternoon dance class, one of the instructors played a song I had never heard before. The song captured my spirit I could not get the melody out of my head. I ran over to her, and asked the name of the song, she had just played. She was somewhat startled since she had never really heard me speak before. "Do you like that music," she asked. The look in my eyes caused her to believe she had caused a crack in my shell. She told me the name of the song was Exodus and the meaning of the song was to live free. I knew within my being this was the music I needed to dance too. I wanted freedom to dance and to be accepted for me. As soon as my mother got home, I asked her about buying me a record with the song Exodus on it. I told her what was going on at the school, and I had less than two weeks to make up a dance to the music I had selected. She did not have the money or the transportation to get the music, but she did call my father and gave him the information. The following weekend my father came over with a bag in his hands. It was a 33 1/3 playing album with the recording of Hollywood's greatest themes. The fifth recording on that album was the theme from The Exodus. That Sunday evening when the house was quiet, I played the album, sat in front of my mirror, and then made some movements in my mind. The moves I made in my mind where spectacular, I felt they would have to accept me. From that day, I developed my own steps and movements. The music seem to captivate every part of my body, it seem as if I floated with the changes in the music. I kept my routine a secret, trying to improve daily with each secret practice session in my mirror. Sharon grew more curious as each day went by, questioning my music and movements; I felt she was more nervous for me than I was for myself. It was the mirror in the foyer that kept my secret as I danced alone each night in the mirror, before my mother came home.

The Monday, two days before the dance I went to Miss Berkley's to remind her of our appointment on Wednesday, and she reminded me to study hard for the school testing, and the audition. She told me the group would be meeting in the gym. The group had never met in the gym to my knowledge, that place was huge, and it was the place I had previous embarrassments with the balance beams and falling down in front of my class.

Tuesday the whole school was talking about my upcoming audition, it was as if someone was selling papers on the corner. The whispers in the hall grew even louder, and some people actually questioned my sanity. One teacher gave me a pat on the back for trying as I passed by his class.

Wednesday finally came and I dreaded the school bell at 3pm. I was so frightened I believe I became numb. Every step to the gym locker room was like my last, Sharon met me on the way, and it was nice to have a friend. I went into the girl's locker room to put on my leotard, with my record in hand. I had not realized the gym was packed to capacity with students and teachers. The girls from the dance group were also in the locker room no one said a word to me. Today I paid no attention to how I looked, I did not even check my hair. I walked out into the gym, and along the wall of the gym, students and teachers filled every space, I saw Sharon and used her as my focus. I slowly walked over to Miss Berkley, gave her the album, and asked if she would play number five. I walked to the middle of the floor and assumed a kneeling position, as the music began to play, I slowly rose to my feet and rose on my toes. In addition, I spun around to the right and to the left. I went into a lunge rolling my body around leaning completely forward. I rolled my arms like a swan, executed some leaps, and finished a few more jumps. As the music quieted down, I made my body soft, expressing myself as if I was floating, using my hands to express softness. I kept a serious look on my face, and as the music, got louder, my steps and movements became bolder. I wanted to express to Miss Berkeley my version of freedom. I would run across the room and suddenly stopped. The motion of my face and hands resembled bonds being broken. As the music began to climax I jumped in the air and came down in a split, and curled up on the floor as if I died, covered my face with my arms and returned to a kneeling position. When I got up the crowd looked shocked, but not Sharon, she started jumping up and down, than the crowd started to cheer too. I walked over to Miss Berkley; she looked at me then signaled one of the dance groups to come to the record player. Miss Berkley asked me to dance with her to the same music, she did her interpretation of the music and I repeated some of my routine, the crowd continued clapping. After the dance, Miss Berkley told me I would be accepted into the group, and to be at rehearsals next Monday after school. Sharon and I walked home together; she told me how proud she was of me. The next week I was at rehearsal with the Magnificent Seven and had to learn their routines quickly. One month later, my first recital came with the group, I was at the end of the line, and I did not mind my position at all. At the end of the program, I heard one of the students in the audience comment, "that group, could really dance especially that dark skinned girl at the end of the line." The Magnificent Seven never really let me know if I was accepted or not. I attempted to do my best when I rehearsed or performed with them. I guess all they wanted from me, was to keep up the group's excellent performance record.

The next week, Miss Berkley asked me to have my parents come to the school for a conference, I began to think this could not be a good thing. I thought I would probably have to repeat sixth grade. Instead, the meeting was about me, but for a different purpose. Miss Berkley told my parents she felt I had a natural gift for dancing, and she was recommending me to Peabody Conservatory of Music for ballet training. She told my parents she felt this might help me in many ways, besides developing my talent. She also told my parents she believed she could obtain a dance scholarship for me. My mother hugged me for a long time with tears in her eyes, and told me how proud she was of me. My father expressed his feelings as well, and took my mother and me to my favorite sub shop for a chicken liver sub, to celebrate the victory. To me a silent victory was to have both my parents together with me, a family. In about a week's time my mother received the paper work from Peabody Conservatory of Music, and began the process of filling the papers out. My father took me down to the Conservatory, it was very beautiful, and I was to start in the summer as soon as school let out.

The next week was the final examination that teachers all over the city had prepared their students to take. I'm pretty sure there were probably students like me, who feared not graduating. When the day finally came, Miss Berkley handed the papers out to each student, when she came to my desk she asked had I registered for Peabody yet. I told her when I was to start, and she answered good and continued handing the examination out. The following week was nerve racking, the whole sixth-grade floor was like a graveyard very quiet, very little joking or laughter, even the teachers seemed very concerned. The test scores had been received, and each individual child was called up to the teacher's desk and told they had passed or was given a letter to take home to their parents. When my turned came to go to the desk, I believe I left my stomach in my chair. Miss Berkley looked at me and said when you go to junior high this year please keep on dancing. I returned to my seat with a smile bigger than my face, and as it turns out our whole class would be graduating. That summer my mother lost her house and the new owners placed a large red sign on the door, with the words auction on it. She had tried her best, working three jobs, but sometimes, things need to work out that way in order for us to travel a new direction. Somehow, despite my mother's financial state, she managed to buy another house that summer in the northwest part of the city. An area where white people had lived, but now too many negroes where moving in so, houses where selling like hot cakes, and my mother managed to get a deal on an end house, semidetached.

We had no furniture just beds to sleep in, and I did not care, even though the neighborhood children questioned on several occasions why we moved in with no furniture. I felt like a princess, I was attending the Peabody Conservatory of Music, to dance, and nothing else mattered. That summer began with instructions from my mother on how to get the transit bus to Peabody. She got on the bus with me, showed me where to transfer to the second bus and to get back to my new house. When my mother taught you, she expected you to listen and get it. The next day, I was on my own, I caught the bus and arrived safely at Peabody, I got there one hour early just to make sure I was not late. I sat down on the wooden benches provided outside of each class. The building was made of wood and on the various floors; one could hear the different voices and instruments playing. Some violins, horns of all kinds, trumpets, just gently complementing each other, no conflicting sounds, then came the voices, sopranos, altos, tenors all in perfect harmony. All of these sounds bouncing off the wooden floors and ceilings, made an echo that seemed to last forever. The memory of that first day, the feeling of accomplishment, and the joy of hearing a different type of world. All the different types of music has always stayed with me.

I attended the Peabody Conservatory of Music for years, until my body began to change, it was a difficult road, and there were some hard ships, dealing with racism, but that did not affect me. I had developed some confidence in myself. I continued to dance until my first year in college. When I encountered a different type of dance instructor, she let it be known that she was not so thrilled with my leaps or ballet performance. She wanted me to concentrate on modern dance not ballet. From then on, I decided to concentrate on my major and leave dancing to other smaller framed girls.

For thirty-six years, this was only a memory, which I kept to myself. I had grown up and had three children of my own. Until one day I took my youngest to the airport and he was running late. He was about to miss his flight when one of the ticket agents recognized me, to my surprise she was one of the Magnificent Seven. She quickly processed his ticket and we ran down to the gate were his plane was to depart. As we were running, she turned to me and asked if I still danced. My response of course was no, than she turned to my son and said "your mother was quite a dancer." That was the first time one of them had made any comment about my dancing. I walked my son to the plane with a new peace in my spirit. I had been accepted long ago and had their respect but never knew it. It was no longer the Magnificent Seven but now it was the Magnificent Eight.

Printed in the United States
By Bookmasters